EPHESIANS

PRECISION THINKING FOR ACCURATE THEOLOGY

Randy White

Copyright © 2019 Randy White
Cover and Illustration: Leonardo Costa
Cover and Illustrations © 2019 DispensationalPublishing House, Inc.

All rights reserved. This book or any portion thereof may not be reproduced or used in any manner whatsoever without the express written permission of the publisher except for the use of brief quotations in a book review.

Scriptures quoted as KJV are taken from the KING JAMES VERSION (KJV).

Printed in the United States of America
First Edition, First Printing, 2018
ISBN: 978-1-945774-32-4

Dispensational Publishing House, Inc.
220 Paseo del Pueblo Norte
Taos, NM 87571

www.dispensationalpublishing.com

Ordering Information: Quantity sales. Special discounts are available on quantity purchases by churches, associations, and others. For details, contact the publisher at the address above.

Orders by U.S. trade bookstores and wholesalers. Please contact the publisher:
Tel: (844) 321-4202

1 2 3 4 5 6 7 8 9 10

*To grammar teachers everywhere who don't know
they are creating future dispensationalists!*

Table of Contents

Preface 1

Ephesians 1:1-3 | The Greeting.. 3

Ephesians 1:4-12 | God's Blessings on Israel 7

Ephesians 1:13-23 | God's Work Among the Gentiles 13
    Comparing God's Work 21
    An overview and proof of pronoun importance 22

Ephesians 2:1-7 | You, Us, and Us Together 27

Ephesians 2:8-10 | Grace and Works and Eternal Purpose................ 31

Ephesians 2:11-22 | God Brings Two Peoples Together 33

Ephesians 3:1-2 | Paul Given a New Dispensation 39

Ephesians 3:3-6 | The Revelation of the Mystery 43

Ephesians 3:7-12 | Paul, the Apostle of the Mystery.......................... 47

Ephesians 3:13-21 | Paul's Desire and Prayer 51

Ephesians 4:1-3 | The Instructions for a Worthy Walk..................... 55

Ephesians 4:4-6 | The Unity of our Bond 57

Ephesians 4:7-16 | The Grace Given for the Unity of our Faith 59

Ephesians 4:17-32 | Practical Instructions for our Walk 63

Ephesians 5:1-14 | Moral Christian Behavior 71

Ephesians 5:15-21 | The Believer's Spiritual Walk............................. 79

Ephesians 5:22-33 | The Believer's Marriage Relationship 83

Ephesians 6:1-4 | The Responsibility of Believing Children and Parents 89

Ephesians 6:5-9 | The Responsibility of Believing Servants and Masters...........91

Ephesians 6:10-18 | The Armor of God 95

Ephesians 6:19-20 | Prayer for Paul 99

Ephesians 6:21-24 | Closing Words..101

PREFACE

The letter to the Ephesians, along with the book of Acts, are the two New Testament books that solidified my understanding of this dispensation more than any other books of the Bible.

I still remember struggling with Calvinism, trying to grapple with the passages of Scripture which clearly speak of predestination. I had surmised that election might be *national* and related to *Israel* rather than *individual* and related to the *church*. I scheduled a lunch appointment with a seminary professor to try out this theory and it was quickly shot down. When I said, "could election be about Israel and not about the church?" he immediately replied, "No, because of Ephesians 1:5."

Well, he had me there. It did say that God **predestinated us**, right there in black and white. There was no way around it, it seemed.

But I still wasn't comfortable with the Calvinistic scheme which removes free will, demands regeneration prior to any expression of faith or acceptance of Christ, creates a monstrous God who creates some men, women, boys and girls in order to damn them to hellfire for His glory, and makes evangelism nothing more than an exercise in obedience. This doesn't even touch the fact that many Scriptures are as decidedly *non-Calvinist* as Ephesians 1:5 seems to be Calvinist.

So I continued the struggle, and in doing so decided I needed to study the letter to the Ephesians word-by-word. And when I did so, SHAZHAM! I discovered the truth that I knew must be there somewhere, and it was as bright as the light of day. What I discovered was that *the pronouns of the letter to the Ephesians place predestination on the nation of Israel and not on the church.*

How could I (and every preacher and commentary I had ever heard or read) not have noticed the difference between the first person plural (us) and the second person plural (you) and not have differentiated these as two separate groups of people? These words never mean the same people in regular language use. Why would they mean the same group in Ephesians 1? And if they don't mean the same people, who was the *us* who was predestined in Ephesians 1:5?

What follows on these pages is my study. The pages are not a commentary, but have commentary. They are a detailed outline that can be used for teaching, personal study, or sermon preparation. You can also find the original video of these lessons as I taught them, which will have added insight, at www.randywhiteministries.org.

Because of the precision of the pronouns in this epistle, I have chosen to subtitle this study *Precision Thinking for Accurate Theology*. I hope you enjoy the journey.

In this book, bold print is used as notation of direct quotes from the King James Version. When the KJV uses italics, the italics are retained in this book. Italics that are not in bold print are simply the author's emphasis.

Randy White,
Taos, NM

EPHESIANS 1:1-3
THE GREETING

- Verse 1 - A close reading of this verse alerts the reader to the fact that Paul is writing to two groups of people: the saints and the faithful. He is not writing to the saints who are faithful (as in NASB). We will build the case that the saints are Jewish believers in the church and the faithful in Christ Jesus are Gentile believers.

- Verse 2 - **Grace** and **peace** is Paul's standard prayer for the recipients of his letter. These two blessings are so aligned with this dispensation, and are the opposite of the plan of God outlined in the prophets in which God promised *judgment and war* when the Jewish nation rejected Him.

- Verse 3 –
    - In verses 3-12, Paul uses the first person plural (us/we).
    - Whereas almost every Bible commentary assumes that this pronoun includes the reader, such an interpretation is neither insisted upon in the text nor logically concluded (or even allowed) from Paul's use of the second person plural (ye/you) beginning in verse 12.

- In verses 13-14 Paul uses both second person and first person, and any logical conclusion must be that Paul speaks of two different groups of people.
- Note that the interpretation of the book of Ephesians must include this change of person.
- The task of the Bible student, then, is to determine the identity of the **us** to whom **all spiritual blessings in heavenly *places* in Christ** have been given. The student can do this by personal evaluation (which is worthless) or asking their pastor (which is equally worthless, if the pastor answers based on his personal evaluation), or by searching the Scriptures to find the recipients of **all spiritual blessings**.
- Who are the recipients of such blessings? Consider the following passages: Genesis 12:2-3, 22:18, Isaiah 61:6-9 , 62:1-2 (note the contrast to the Gentiles in both Isaiah passages), Romans 3:1-2.
- The only rational conclusion is that the *Jews of faith* are "us" in verses 3-12. This will mean that non-Jews of faith (i.e.: Gentile believers) are the "ye" beginning in v. 13.
- If one concludes that *us* is "the church," then who will "ye" be? Was Paul so sloppy in grammar and speech as to simply use the wrong pronoun, or do the pronouns convey precise spiritual information?
- Most Bible translations make a subtle insertion into Ephesians 1 that leads the student on a "wild goose chase" by pre-setting their focus.
    - NASB inserts a heading: The Blessings of Redemption
    - ESV/NRSV/GNB/NIV inserts a heading: Spiritual Blessings in Christ
    - The ESV contains an introduction to the book of Ephesians, and the first sentence says, "The apostle Paul wrote Ephesians

to the churches around Ephesus (Acts 19) to display the scope of God's eternal plan for all humanity—for Jews and Gentiles alike. This is the mystery of God, hidden for ages but now made known in Jesus Christ."[1]

- NOTE: The "scope of God's eternal plan for humanity" is not the mystery of God, hidden for ages. From at least Genesis 12:3 it is abundantly obvious that the scope of "God's eternal plan for humanity" included "Jews and Gentiles alike." Such a statement is either spiritually ignorant or so enamored with a personal theological agenda as to call it Biblical malpractice.

---

[1] The Holy Bible: English Standard Version (Wheaton: Standard Bible Society, 2016), Eph.

EPHESIANS 1:4-12
GOD'S BLESSINGS ON ISRAEL

- ▸ Verse 4 –

  - Our interpretation of v. 3 should be confirmed in the pronouns of v. 4 (and beyond). If, therefore, the Jewish believers are "us," then do the descriptions of vv. 4-12 align with this interpretation?

  - Who, then, has been **chosen...in him before the foundation of the world** to be **holy and without blame before him**? For the answer, consider Deuteronomy 7:6-7, Psalm 33:12, 135:4, Isaiah 41:8, 65:8-10, Matthew 24:22, 24, 31, 1 Peter 1:1-2, etc.

  - Were the Jews chosen to **be holy and without blame**? See Leviticus 19:2, Isaiah 26:2, 1 Peter 1:16, 1 Peter 2:9, etc.

- ▸ Verse 5 –

  - Are the Jews those who are **predestinated...unto the adoption of children**? The standard Reformed Theology conclusion is that God has predestined certain people to be adopted as His children and left the rest to be damned. Is such a conclusion merited here?

- Consider Romans 9:4 -
    - There is not a single passage in the Bible that gives **the adoption** to all believers. Rather, this is a matter that is related to Israel, as this passage unequivocally declares.
    - The believers of Israel currently have the **Spirit of adoption** (Rom. 8:15) but are **waiting for the adoption** itself (Rom. 8:23).
    - Galatians 4:5 also restricts the **adoption of sons** to those who **were under the law**.
- While most Christian theologians consider adoption to be part of general Christian doctrine in the church-age, such a theology doesn't align with this verse, nor the others about adoption.
    - By surmising that adoption is *being brought into a new family*, they then proceed with eisegesis to prove their assumption.
    - However, adoption as sons is not *being brought into a new family* but is about a son who was *born into the family* receiving the legal right to manage the affairs of the household.
    - In the church age, we are not born into the family and later receive full rights. Rather, we are gifted eternal life by grace through faith, and receive the full rights of the relationship immediately.

▸ Verse 6 –

- The Reformed/Calvinist position works overtime to claim that my predestination and your damnation is **to the praise of the glory of his grace**. I fail to see the praiseworthiness of such a doctrine, or the graciousness of the same.
- However, if the Jewish nation is in view, then His selection of this nation is **to the praise of the glory of his grace**, because it does not involve the damnation of others, as is inherently necessary in Calvinism.

- Has (or will) God made Israel to be **accepted in the beloved**? (The verb allows for either a past tense or a future tense interpretation). Consider Isaiah 45:25 and Jeremiah 23:6.
▸ Verse 7 - The Jewish nation has **redemption through his blood**. It has not yet *received* this redemption, but the redemption is promised to the nation (see Zech. 9:11 and Rom. 11:26).
▸ Verse 8 –
  - In the grace of God, the Jewish people became the recipients of *abounding* **wisdom and prudence**.
    ○ The word **prudence** is φρόνησις [phronesis], based on *phren*, a word related to mental ability and understanding.
  - Hebrews 6:4-5 (interpreted correctly as a message to the Jewish nation) gives this same testimony.
  - Romans 3:1-2 also speaks of the abundance of wisdom and knowledge that was given to the Jewish nation.
▸ Verses 9-10 –
  - These verses are related to verse 8. The **wisdom and prudence** which has **abounded toward** the Jewish nation is most evident in that to them God has **made known...the mystery of his will**.
  - This is not, in my opinion, the mystery of the church age (which was *not* made known to the Jewish nation, but rather to Paul when he was *outside* the Jewish nation).
  - Rather, the mystery spoken of here is that in the dispensation of the fullness of times he might gather together in one all things in Christ.
    ○ This dispensation is a yet-future time when **all things** will be **together...in Christ**, including all things **in heaven, and which are on earth**.

- This is not descriptive of our day, but is descriptive of the coming Messianic Kingdom.
- Most modern versions have shown themselves allergic to the word *dispensation:*
  - The ESV says "a plan for the fullness of time," though the Greek has no connection to plans and planning.
  - The NASB refers to "an administration suitable to the fullness of the times." While "administration" is closer, it is not as clear as *dispensation.* The HCSB also uses "administration."
  - The NIV avoids the term altogether, saying, "the mystery... to put into effect when the times reach their fulfillment."

▶ Verse 11 –

- The grammatical structure of the sentence is: being predestined in Christ (according to the purpose of him who worketh all things according to the counsel of his will), we obtained an inheritance.
- It has already been determined in verses 4-5 that the **being predestinated** is something that concerns the Jewish nation. This can be further verified in v. 11 by asking, who has obtained an inheritance by predestination?
- Compare Galatians 3:14-18, especially 18.
  - The Jewish nation has been given an *inheritance of promise,* not based on Law whatsoever.
  - While *possession of the land* was based on law, *inheritance of the land* was based on promise.
  - Romans 4:13-14 solidifies this argument.
- Some Calvinists use the last phrase of the verse (**who worketh all things after the counsel of his own will**) to build a fatalist

worldview on every event and occurrence of life. This is making the phrase say more than it actually says. God does work **all things after the counsel of his own will**, but it does not follow that, "There are no accidents in your life. Nothing has been left to chance. Every economic downturn, every phone call in the middle of the night, every oncology report has been sent to us from the God who sees all things, plans all things, and loves us more than we know" (Kevin DeYoung, https://www.thegospelcoalition.org/blogs/kevin-deyoung/all-things-in-fact/).

- The **counsel of his own will** and the *direct work of God's hand* are not the same.

▶ Verse 12 –

- The purpose of being predestinated to an inheritance (v. 11) is so that the Jewish nation should be **to the praise of his glory**.
- The reference is to **we...who first trusted in Christ**.
    - This phrase is very important in determining the identity of the first person plural used in vv. 3-11.
    - There is no conceivable way in which the Ephesians were the first to trust in Christ. It is only the Jewish believers of Jerusalem who were the first to trust in Christ (See Jn. 1:49, Matt. 16:16, Jn. 12:13, etc.).

EPHESIANS 1:13-23
GOD'S WORK AMONG THE GENTILES

▶ Verse 13 –

- In verses 13-23, the second person plural pronoun (ye/you/your) is used 11 times, while in vv. 3-12 it is not used at all. In vv. 3-12 the first person plural is used nine times, while in vv. 13-13 it is used only three times.

  ○ Any interpretation of vv. 3-23 (and beyond) that does not have regard for this sudden change in person is incomplete and inadequate (if not irresponsible).

  ○ Does Paul make the switch between "us" and "you" haphazardly or by mistake?

  ○ This is strengthened further by the fact that Paul says **ye also**, using the Greek καί [kai], which is an adverb contrasting the *we* from the *ye*.

- Notice that there were those **who first trusted in Christ** (v. 12) and then **ye also** *trusted*, so it is impossible that the **we... who first trusted** are the Ephesians, who **also** *trusted*, but at a later date.

- The trust came **after that ye heard the word of truth, the gospel of your salvation**. Two things are noteworthy.
  - First, trust always comes after hearing, for **faith *cometh* by hearing, and hearing by the word of God** (Rom. 10:17).
    - The adage, "share the gospel, and use words when necessary" is false (and falsely attributed to Francis of Assisi).
    - The gospel cannot be shared with anything other than words because the gospel is not *love that can be displayed* but *logic that must be accepted*.
  - Second, Paul speaks of the gospel of your salvation.
    - There is (contrary to common opinion) more than one *gospel*, though there is only one name by which we must be saved (Acts 4:12).
    - The Gospel of the Kingdom, for example was that **the kingdom of God is at hand** and thus the Jewish nation should **repent ye, and believe the gospel** (Mark 1:14-15, where **the gospel** could not have included the death, burial, and resurrection of Jesus Christ, for such had not occurred nor did *anyone* believe that it would occur).
- After having believed, the Gentiles were **sealed with that holy Spirit of promise**. The sealing is mentioned again in Ephesians 4:30.
  - In Revelation 7:2 the 144,000 are sealed, and this sealing gives them total protection from the tribulation.
  - If the "physical" sealing of the 144,000 resulted in the total protection of the body, we can assume that a "spiritual" sealing results in total protection of the soul.

- Verse 14 –

  - Here Paul reverts to the first person plural, speaking of **our inheritance**.
  - This is theologically sound, because the church does not have an **inheritance**, but rather has a *free gift*.
  - The Greek κληρονομία [klaronomia] is *the designation of the law*, thus, inheritance (that which the law designates as yours). Only the nation of Israel has an inheritance.
  - Notice that Paul said **we have obtained an inheritance** in v. 11, thus now speaks of **our inheritance** rather than *your inheritance*.
  - The Holy Spirit, who has sealed the church in salvation, is **the earnest** of the **inheritance** until **the redemption of the purchased possession**.
    - The word **redemption** is ἀπολύτρωσις [apolytrosis] which has the word *ransom* as its root. That is, there is a *ransom payment* for that which had already been purchased.
    - The idea that God had purchased Israel is given in Exodus 15:16, Deuteronomy 32:6, 2 Samuel 7:23, and Psalm 74:2, among others.

- Verse 15 –

  - Once again, the Ephesians could not have been the first who **trusted in Christ** (v. 12) because here Paul hears of their faith at a later date.
  - In addition to hearing of their faith, Paul heard of their **love unto all the saints**. That is, Paul is rejoicing that the Ephesian gentiles love the Jewish believers.

- Verses 16-17 –

  - Paul was so overjoyed with **having heard of your faith…and love unto all the saints** (v. 15) that he did not **cease…to give thanks** for the Ephesian believers, also **making mention** of them in his prayers.

  - The word **mention** is μνεία [mneia], from which we get *amnesia* (the lack of memory) and *hypermnesia* (a memory far beyond normal). Thus it could be interpreted, *making effort to never forget to pray for you.*

  - His prayer was that the Ephesians would have **the spirit of wisdom and revelation in the knowledge of him**. Note that **the knowledge of him** is foundational, and that God would add to this knowledge a **spirit of wisdom and revelation**, that is, a proper application and understanding of the knowledge. This spirit is further explained in vv. 18-19.

- Verse 18 –

  - This verse is part of the spirit of **wisdom and revelation** of the previous verse. Having this spirit is a result of the **eyes of your understanding** being enlightened.

    - Once again we see that **eyes of understanding** are not opened by a mystical experience, but by the light of knowledge, which is, in this case, spiritual knowledge.

    - A spiritual mindset is required to recognize spiritual truth, but a mystical experience is not required (see 1 Cor. 2:12-14).

  - Paul's prayer is that this enlightenment would lead the Christian to the knowledge and understanding of **the hope of his calling** as well as **the riches of the glory of his inheritance.** Do we know what these two things even are?

- First, the hope of his calling:
  - It is a reference to God's calling.
  - The Greek word has a wide variety of uses, and the root is used 517 times, meaning everything from "named" (Matt. 1:21) to "invited" (Lk. 14:7-24).
  - The call is something that is clearly given to church-age believers in this passage, along with Ephesians 4:1, 4:4, and 2 Thessalonians 1:11.
  - The call is given to both Jews and Gentiles (1 Cor. 7:18-20), while election is exclusively of the Jewish *nation* (not individuals). Compare also Matthew 22:14.
  - The calling of God is **without repentance** (i.e. irrevocable) - Romans 11:29.
  - Though it lends itself to the Calvinist argument, it does not require an individual/unconditional election (see 1 Tim. 6:12, for example, which implies that there is a necessary response to the call).
  - The **hope** of the calling is blessings of the invitation.
  - Translation note: The ESV says "hope to which he has called you." This displays the Calvinistic bias given in the ESV, and is not supported by the Greek. Note that the two phrases following use the same genitive construction, "The riches of the glory," and "the exceeding greatness of his power." To change this first phrase to meet a preconceived theological agenda is interpretive malpractice.
- Second, the riches of the glory of his inheritance in the saints.

- Note that God's inheritance is **in the saints**. To determine the identity of the saints, allow Scripture to interpret itself. At least 38 passages speak of God's inheritance, including Deuteronomy 32:9, Psalm 28:9, and Psalm 33:12. If Israel is His inheritance, then **his inheritance in the saints** is equivalent to *His inheritance in Israel*.

- Paul's prayer is that Gentile believers would know the **glory of his inheritance** in Israel, yet most Gentile believers do not even believe that Israel is His inheritance. Consider these quotes:

    - ✓ "Just as Canaan was Israel's inheritance, and Hebron was the best of Canaan, so it is with the church which is the greatest of all the things that Christ will inherit."[2]

    - ✓ "Yes. We are God's inheritance. The God who created and who rules the entire universe has in inheritance in us. Let's get to work for God here on earth so we can give Him the inheritance in us that he deserves, shall we?"[3]

    - ✓ "You are a beloved child of God; you are the heir of God's inheritance."[4]

    - ✓ "The idea that God, by His grace, makes us into His inheritance is incredible."[5]

---

2 (http://www.livingwaters.cl/magazine/19/02.htm)

3 Janna Rust, (2007, May) God's inheritance. [Blog Post]. Retrieved from https://jannascrumbs.typepad.com/bread_crumbs/2007/05/index.html

4 Charles F. Stanley, *Discovering Your Identity*. (Nashville, Tennessee: Thomas Nelson, 2008).

5 R.C. Sproul, (n.d.) God's inheritance. [Blog Post]. Retrieved from https://www.ligonier.org/learn/devotionals/providence-and-gods-inheritance/

- Verse 19 –
  - Paul adds a third thing to his detail concerning his prayer for **the spirit of wisdom and revelation in the knowledge of him** (v. 17).
    - He wants the gentile believers to know **the exceeding greatness of his power to us-ward who believe**.
    - While the us-ward could be all-inclusive, it makes more sense to see it as it has been throughout the letter, the transition of *you* and *us* being a contrast between *Gentile believer* and *Jewish believer*.
      - This is especially true since he has used the second person in vv. 17-18 and now suddenly switches to the first person.
      - If he meant *us* all the way through, why didn't he use *us* all the way through?
      - In simplifying the sentence, it becomes even more clear, as Paul prays **that ye may know** (v. 18)... **what is the exceeding greatness of his power to us-ward**.
      - Note that he doesn't say, "that we may know," using a consistent first person, but moves from "you" to "us."
      - Theologically, this fits perfectly with Paul's prayer that the Gentile believers would now **the glory of his inheritance in the saints**, but especially the **exceeding greatness** toward the *believing saints*.
  - Either the **greatness of his power** is **according to the working of his mighty power** (a somewhat redundant statement, but possible), or Paul is praying **that ye may know** (v. 18) by **the working of his mighty power**, thus this last phrase being more

inclusive. Both grammatically and logically it seems more plausible that Paul is praying that his entire prayer would be answered in God's **mighty power**.

▸ Verse 20 - The **mighty power** of God was **wrought in Christ**.

- The word **wrought** is the past tense of *work* (the formula still used in words like *catch*, *bring*, and *teach*), thus **wrought** is "worked," and is based on the Greek word ἐνεργέω [energeo], thus has the implication of the exertion of energy.

- God's power was *worked* in Christ at the resurrection, and then displayed at the ascension.

▸ Verse 21 –

- This verse describes the current location and status of Jesus Christ.

- He is **far above** every ἀρχή [arche] (ruler) and ἐξουσία [exousia] (power of authority) and δύναμις [dunamis] (power of might) and κυριότης [kuriotes] (lordship / domain) and **every name that is named** in all αἰών [aion] (ages).

- Therefore, though Jesus is not on the throne of David (but currently at God's **right hand** (v. 20), He is nonetheless the all-powerful *coming* King.

▸ Verse 22 –

- This does not testify that the Kingdom has begun. Notice that the church sees this not in reality, but in spirituality (v. 18). Note Hebrews 2:8 and 1 Corinthians 15:23-25.

- This simply expresses what Christ expressed in Matthew 28:18, "all authority has been given to me."

- The last phrase should read, *and gave him, the head over all, to the church* (that is, remove the translator's insertions).

- ▸ Verse 23 - This is a powerful word about the church, described as **his body** and His **fullness**.
  - Note that this either refers to the local church or the local church is incomplete in itself (and thus should not be "independent").
  - The requirements for "a church" must be the requirements for "the church."
    - "A church" has ordinances (Baptism and the Lord's Supper), but the so-called universal church 1) cannot determine what the meaning of these ordinance are, and 2) limits these ordinances to the local church.
    - "A church" has Biblical leadership (Elders / Deacons), but "the church" would have no agreement as to its leadership.
    - If it doesn't have the elements of a church, it is not "church."

Comparing God's Work

God's work among the Jews	God's work among the Gentiles
Every spiritual blessing in the heavenlies – v. 3	Having believed, were sealed with the Spirit – v. 13
Chosen…to be holy – v. 4	Can receive the spirit of wisdom and revelation in the knowledge of God – v. 17
Predestined to adoption as sons – v. 5	Enjoy "the hope of his calling" – v. 18
Made accepted in Jesus – v. 6	Can rejoice in the riches of God's future inheritance – v. 18

God's work among the Jews	God's work among the Gentiles
Promised redemption in His blood – v. 7	–
Given abundance of wisdom and prudence – v. 8	–
Given the mystery of the future "fullness of times" – vv. 10-11	–
Given an inheritance – v. 11	–
Were the first to trust Christ – v. 12	–
Enjoy the "exceeding greatness of His power" (v. 19)	–

An overview and proof of pronoun importance

▸ A summary glance at Ephesians 2 shows that the pronoun changes are…

- Of fundamental importance
- Of theological precision
- Of the nature that they must be explained and cannot be ignored.

▸ The following displays different focus between first person plural (we/us, etc.) and second person plural (ye/you, etc.)

First Person	Second Person	Insights
	1 And you hath he quickened, who were dead in trespasses and sins; 2 Wherein in time past ye walked according to the course of this world, according to the prince of the power of the air, the spirit that now worketh in the children of disobedience	It was the gentile people who walked according to the course of this world
3 Among whom also we all had our conversation in times past in the lusts of our flesh, fulfilling the desires of the flesh and of the mind; and were by nature the children of wrath, even as others. 4 But God, who is rich in mercy, for his great love wherewith he loved us, 5 Even when we were dead in sins, hath quickened us together with Christ,	(by grace ye are saved;)	Paul has moved from "you" (vv. 1-2) to "we" (v. 3) and "us" (v. 4). Either he is unbelievably bad at grammar (and the Holy Spirit inspired bad grammar) or these changes of pronoun have meaning. Paul further gives a parenthetical statement that switches from "us" (vv 4-5a) to "ye" (v. 5b), then back to "us" again (v. 6). This switch has to have meaning.

First Person	Second Person	Insights
6 And hath raised us up together, and made us sit together in heavenly places in Christ Jesus: 7 That in the ages to come he might shew the exceeding riches of his grace in his kindness toward us through Christ Jesus.	8 For by grace are ye saved through faith; and that not of yourselves: it is the gift of God: 9 Not of works, lest any man should boast.	Paul reverts to "ye" in verse 8, coming back to his parenthetical statement of v. 5b.
10 For we are his workmanship, created in Christ Jesus unto good works, which God hath before ordained that we should walk in them.	11 Wherefore remember, that ye being in time past Gentiles in the flesh, who are called Uncircumcision by that which is called the Circumcision in the flesh made by hands; 12 That at that time ye were without Christ, being aliens from the commonwealth of Israel, and strangers from the covenants of promise, having no hope, and without God in the world: 13 But now in Christ Jesus ye who sometimes were far off are made nigh by the blood of Christ.	

First Person	Second Person	Insights
14 For he is our peace, who hath made both one, and hath broken down the middle wall of partition between us; 15 Having abolished in his flesh the enmity, even the law of commandments contained in ordinances; for to make in himself of twain one new man, so making peace; 16 And that he might reconcile both unto God in one body by the cross, having slain the enmity thereby:	17 And came and preached peace to you which were afar off, and to them that were nigh.	While verses 14-16 speak of both groups, they do so from the reference point of the Jews; Paul speaks of the law of commandments, no doubt a reference to the Mosaic Law, and only relevant for the Jews. In verse 17 the first reference is to those afar off. Both groups enjoy the peace of the reconciliation in Christ, as is seen clearly in verse 18.
18 For through him we both have access by one Spirit unto the Father.		
	19 Now therefore ye are no more strangers and foreigners, but fellow citizens with the saints, and of the household of God; 20 And are built upon the foundation of the apostles and prophets, Jesus Christ himself being the chief corner stone; 21 In whom all the building fitly framed together groweth unto an holy temple in the Lord: 22 In whom ye also are builded together for an habitation of God through the Spirit.	If the saints are all believers, then how have the gentiles suddenly become fellow citizens with the saints? Under the standard evangelical definition, it would have been better to say, but now ye are saints. In the terminology used, the Ephesians and the saints are not the same people.

EPHESIANS 2:1-7
YOU, US, AND US TOGETHER

Paul speaks of some things that are true for **you** (the gentiles) and also true of **us** (the Jews) and thus are true of **us together**, both Jews and Gentiles.

▶ Verse 1 –

- The verb *hath he quickened* is borrowed for the completion of the sentence in v. 5. However, grammatically it could just as readily be **he loved** from v. 4 (both thoughts would be theologically correct, so no change of doctrine is effected).

- Do not be taken in by the oft-given remark that *dead people cannot do anything*. This argument is created by Calvinists to "prove" that a sinner cannot accept Jesus Christ without first being regenerated by election. However, the sentence grammatically is connected with v. 2, saying, *ye walked, being dead*. The death spoken of is not the inability to make choices, it is the deadness in which the unsaved sinner is living, walking, and breathing.

- Gentiles have been *loved* and *quickened*, but in cannot be deduced that this is a gentile experience alone, for vv. 4-5 conclude that the Jews and Gentiles have had the same experience. Note that since the Jews are the elect nation, the love of God and the quickening work of God is not related to election, thus election must pertain to something else.

▶ Verse 2 - To walk according to the course of this world (which is ruled by the prince of the power of the air) is precisely what people who are dead in trespasses and sins do.

▶ Verse 3 –

- Since Paul has said **ye walked** (in sin), now he says **also we** (walked in sin).
- Both Jews and Gentiles were **children of wrath** (v. 3).
- Many passages confirm that all people, regardless of being Jew or Gentile, are **children of wrath.** Consider-
  - Isaiah 53:6 (which, in context, is about Israel-see Is. 52:1).
  - Daniel 9:5-9 (Daniel's prayer of repentance on behalf of Judah).
  - Romans 1:21-25 (Paul's condemnation of the Gentiles)
  - Summary: Romans 3:9-12.

▶ Verses 4-5 –

- God has displayed **mercy** to the Jewish nation, and the believers of that nation were **quickened...together with Christ.**
- **By grace are ye saved** - Paul jumps ahead in excitement to a topic he will elaborate on in vv. 8-9.

- Verse 6 –
  - Is the Jewish nation (or at least the remnant) **raised...up together** and have they been made to **sit together in heavenly** *places* **in Christ Jesus**?
    - According to Ephesians 1:3 they are blessed with **all spiritual blessings** in the heavenlies.
    - They are given a **heavenly calling** (Heb. 3:1) and have tasted of the **heavenly gift** (Heb. 6:4).
    - The Patriarchs desired a **better** *country,* **that is, an heavenly** (Heb. 11:16). Note that *country* is assumed by translators, just as *places* is in Ephesians 2:6.
    - Jesus often spoke to the Jewish nation about the promise to **sit together**, using illustrations such as a banquet (Lk. 12:37), gave promises of dining together in the Kingdom (Lk. 22:29-30), and promised to drink the fruit of the vine with them in the coming Kingdom (Mt. 26:29).
  - Note that, based on the following verse, this spiritual reality does not equate to the present salvation of the Jewish nation.
  - Note also that Paul often speaks of future realities in "as completed" terms, and also that the Greek does not have a *past* nor a *future* tense.
- Verse 7 –
  - The reason the Jewish nation is raised up and seated in the heavenlies is because of a *future* plan for **the ages to come**.
  - For those who equate the "us" with the church, it is hard to imagine how Christ will show **the exceeding riches of his grace** more to us in the future than He already has. But for the Jewish nation, currently under a partial blindness, the ages to come will be a time in which the Lord displays his **kindness** toward them.

EPHESIANS 2:8-10
GRACE AND WORKS AND ETERNAL PURPOSE

▶ Verses 8-9 –

- To be saved **by grace** is nothing new. Any salvation of any type since the fall is gracious on God's part. To allow Adam to live to see another sunrise was grace.

- However, it is only in this dispensation of grace that salvation of the soul is a gift offered to anyone, anywhere, anytime, solely on the basis of **faith** which is void of **works, lest any man should boast**.

- Is this "dual covenant" theology? (The belief that Jews can be saved under the old covenant today). Not at all!

    - Rather, it is a theology that says that *salvation as we know it* was not offered in previous dispensations.

    - Under the Law, a person was *saved* only when the Kingdom would arrive, and entering that Kingdom would require certain acts of obedience, (repentance, for example).

- ▶ Verse 10 –
    - Either Paul (and therefore God) is duplicitous or verse 10 is not talking about the church.
    - Is it really honest to say, "you are not saved by works but you are saved for works?" If you do not produce, you must then be outside of the boundaries of the purpose of your salvation?
    - Can all our works be "filthy rags" (Is. 64:6) before salvation and **ordained** after salvation?
    - The solution is in the pronouns! The **we** is once again a pronoun for the Jewish nation, which was pre-ordained **unto good works** and is the **workmanship** of God.
        - **His workmanship**: Deuteronomy 32:6, Psalm 100:3, Isaiah 43:21, 44:21, 60:21.
        - **Created…unto good works**: Deuteronomy 5:33.
    - While the *church* was saved (and remains saved) outside of works altogether (Rom. 3:28), the nation of Israel was created to be *the light of the world* and *the salt of the earth*.
    - Could it be that God would ordain (in a Calvinist sense) that certain people would be saved without works and that the sign of this salvation would be works? That they would be saved without works to be ordained to works? This is inconsistent at best.
    - A better view of these verses is that the church (you and me) was saved and remains saved by grace through faith, and that the nation of Israel is ordained to certain good works, which they will someday walk in.

EPHESIANS 2:11-22
GOD BRINGS TWO PEOPLES TOGETHER

- ▸ Verse 11 –
  - The Scriptures use the word ἔθνος [ethnos] carefully, always clarifying when the word signifies those who are not of Israel by referring to them as the **uncircumcision** or otherwise contrasting them to the Jewish people.
    - ○ While the word is often a reference to uncircumcision, one should question that assumption each time the word *gentile* is used.
    - ○ The word *ethnos* is *not* inherently *non-Jewish* and requires interpretation.
    - ○ The word *gentile* is a modern, exclusively non-Jewish word that is not a direct equivalent to *ethnos*.
  - Notice that the pronoun **ye** is given definition here (that confirms our previous conclusion) as being **gentiles**.
    - ○ Notice also that the recipients were **gentiles in the flesh** both before and after the work of God in their lives.
    - ○ The reference to **in times past** has to do with their spiritual reality of being **strangers**, etc., as shown in v. 12.

- Verse 12 –
  - This verse is fundamental to understanding the work of God, and is fundamentally dispensational.
  - There was a time (disregarding the common teaching) in which Gentiles were **aliens** and **strangers** and were therefore **having no hope, and without God in the world**. It is totally impossible to hold to covenant theology (or sloppy dispensationalism) and affirm this verse at the same time.
  - The verse does not say:
    - They did not know where hope was to be found.
    - They had very little hope.
    - They were living without hope (though hope was available to them).
  - Rather, it clearly says that they were totally without hope and without God.
    - It cannot be said of lost people today that they are **having no hope** or **without God in the world**, for the *hope* of *God* has been provided for *all* in Christ Jesus.
    - The lost today may not have recognized or heard of their hope, but there is hope for them!
  - Why were the gentiles previously without hope and without God? Because to have such, they had to be in the **commonwealth of Israel** (the political entity) and within the **covenants of promise** (that were limited to those within the **commonwealth**).
- Verse 13 –
  - The word **sometimes** is the same Greek word translated **in times past** in v. 11. The Gentiles were, *in times past,* **far off** but are now **made nigh** to God, all through **the blood of Christ**.

- Several things are of note:
  - This is said of all Gentiles, not just of select "chosen" Gentiles.
  - The **blood of Christ** was shed in order that Jesus might become **Lord both of the dead and the living** (Rom. 14:9). An added benefit was that this activity made Jesus the **propitiation...for** *the sins of* **the whole world** (1 Jn. 2:2), and therefore the Gentiles were **made nigh**.
  - To be **made nigh** is not to receive salvation, but rather to be given *hope* and the access to God which was once denied to all who were outside of the nation and covenants of Israel.

▶ Verse 14 –

- Sadly, this verse is often used to speak about racial conciliation. This misses the point. While the Bible does speak to racial reconciliation, this verse is not such a passage.
- The Jews and Gentiles were separated by a **middle wall of partition**, and the only real reference to this is the barrier to the Gentiles in the temple.
- Without the blood of Christ, the blood of a sacrifice would be the only provision for the atonement of sin. A Gentile was prohibited from making such a sacrifice by **the middle wall of partition**. By this, he was **without hope** and **without God**.

▶ Verse 15 –

- The word **abolished** is the strongest word available for *removing all energy* - καταργέω [katargeo].
- It is **the law of commandments** *contained* **in ordinances** that was abolished in his flesh, which removed the enmity between man and God.
  - The Law is the Mosaic Law, the Torah.

- Those who try to retain the Law as a rule for Christian living are *legalists* and are teaching that which is unbiblical.
- With the enmity removed, we are now *reconciled* to God (2 Cor. 5:19) and thus can enter into a relationship with Him **by grace...through faith** (v. 8).
- Now, those who receive the gift of salvation are **one new man** that is **in himself**. That is, we are *in Christ* and are therefore *the body of Christ* and His body is both Jew and Gentile, redeemed by the blood!

▶ Verse 16 –

- When Paul teaches that **both** Jew and Gentile are reconciled **into God in one body** he is making reference to the physical, corporeal body of Christ, not the church.
- In the physical body of Christ we have been reconciled unto God. The church does not reconcile, it is a gathering of the reconciled.
- The **enmity** was **slain** by the physical body of Christ (the **enmity** being the same as in v. 15, **the law of commandments** which kept Jew and Gentile separated and kept the Gentile in a position of being without hope).

▶ Verses 17-18 - The work of the physical body of Christ on the cross enabled a proclamation of **peace** to the **afar off** and the **nigh**.

- Note: do not let the pronouns **you** and **them** confuse you. In Greek, it says, "to the far off and to the near," using no pronouns.
- The end result is that now (unlike the previous dispensation) **we both have access...unto the Father**.

▶ Verse 19 –

- A few important insights:

- The Gentiles (**ye**) are no longer without hope and without God.
- They are now **fellow citizens with the saints**. This does not say, *ye are now saints* (as standard evangelicalism teaches).
- Does this mean that Gentiles are now citizens of Israel? They are *fellow citizens of the saints [who are] also of the household of God* (my translation).

- And some thoughts:
  - Would this verse make any sense without dissecting the *we* from the *ye* in chapters 1 & 2?
  - Would it make sense for us to object that Jews had differing privileges from Gentiles in chapter 1, but then argue they have now been made equal in chapter 2?
  - If, as so many teach, there is and has only been "one people of God," then what are these verses about? (A recent social media post: "The Church is Israel. God has one people, not two, always has and always will.")

▶ Verse 20 –

- We (the gentile believers) are **built upon** a foundation that is wholly Jewish, since the **apostles and prophets** were Jewish.
  - It is essential to realize that this is our **foundation** and not the *structure* of the building.
  - Good Christian doctrine would be irrational and unsubstantiated without the revelation and teaching of the Hebrew scriptures and the Gospels. But if you use these to order your daily Christian life, you are living in a different dispensation that does not mix with the current.

- Modern cornerstones are ceremonial, but the ancient cornerstone was the stone that set the direction of all other stones. All prophecy and apostolic work is set in the direction of Jesus Christ and points to Him and is guided by Him.

▶ Verses 21-22 –

- God is building a building which is to be a **holy temple** and a **habitation of God**.
- This aligns with Paul's teaching in 1 Corinthians 3:16 which says, **ye are a temple of God**.
  - Note the plural **ye**. Grammar insists that this is to be understood as teaching that the church is collectively the temple of God rather than each one from among you are individually the temple of God.
  - Ephesians 2:21-22 speaks of the various components of the building being fitly framed together until it groweth into an holy temple in the Lord...for an habitation of God through the Spirit.
- This is a *question the assumptions* matter. Paul certainly had a way of saying *each of you individually are the temple* but he did not use that grammar. See, for example, 1 Corinthians 14:26, comparing the singular with the plural.
- For the greatest proof that it is the *collective local church* that is the temple, consider 1 Corinthians 12:27. I am not the body of Christ, but "we" are the body, and I a member of the body. If I am not the body, am I (individually) the temple?
- Furthermore, 1 Corinthians 6:19 says **your body is the temple** while 1 Corinthians 6:15 (only four verses prior) says **your bodies are the members of Christ**. It would be utterly foolish to argue that when Paul said **your body** in v. 19 that he meant **your bodies**, words which he had just previously used in v. 15.

EPHESIANS 3:1-2
PAUL GIVEN A NEW DISPENSATION

▶ Verse 1 –

- Paul was **the prisoner of Jesus Christ** for "you the nations."
- He was not a *prisoner for* nor a *prisoner because of*, but a **prisoner of**.
- Paul used this same terminology in Ephesians 4:1 and Philemon 1:1, 9, with similar wording in 2 Timothy 1:8.
- While Paul wrote these letters from prison (or house arrest), Paul chooses to emphasize that he is a **prisoner of** rather than a *prisoner for* Jesus Christ. In 1 Corinthians 9:16 he says, **woe unto me if I preach not the Gospel**.

▶ Verse 2 –

- Paul clearly claims to have been given a **dispensation of the grace of God**.
- A **dispensation** is a period under a certain *economy* (thus the Greek *οἰκονομία* [oikonomia]). Every dispensation begins with a revelation that provides fundamentally new information.
- Was this dispensation given to others also?

- It is grammatically possible. However, if it was given to many, the grammar would have made more sense (and have been more transparent) to speak of the dispensation "which is given to you."
- No one else in the New Testament claims to have been given a dispensational mystery.
- Paul repeats this claim often: v. 8, Romans 11:13, 12:3, 15:15-16, 1 Corinthians 9:17, Galatians 1:15-16, 2:8-9, Colossians 1:25, 1 Timothy 1:11, 2:7.
- The testimony of the Lord speaks to this claim: Acts 9:15, 22:21.
- In the end, it would be very hard to claim that this dispensation was given (i.e.: revealed) to others beside Paul, except through Paul.

- When did this dispensation begin?
  - If it indeed came to Paul only, then it could not have begun before Paul.
  - There is no evidence in the Gospels nor the book of Acts that the **dispensation of the grace of God** began before Paul.
  - While *the church* may have begun before Paul, the *church as we know it* began with Paul.[6]

- What are the unique characteristics of this dispensation?
  - It is a dispensation that offers *individual* rather than *national* salvation.

---

[6] I recommend reading James Willingham, *The Church of the New Testament: Considering the Differences Between the Apostolic and the Pauline Assemblies.* (Taos, NM: Dispensational Publishing House, 2018).

- It is unrelated to the Kingdom.
- It has a *Savior* rather than a *Messiah* or *King*.
- Its salvation does not require works and does not allow works. It is fully a gift of God.
- It is available to anyone, anytime, anywhere.

EPHESIANS 3:3-6

THE REVELATION OF THE MYSTERY

▶ Verse 3 –

- The proper understanding of Ephesians 3:3-7 is essential. I am convinced that if one does not understand the mystery that God made known to Paul by revelation, then that person does not have their theology straight, and it will show in their doctrine over and over again.

- A Biblical **mystery** is something that can only be known **by revelation**. After it is revealed, it is no longer a mystery. The dissemination of the information is not a revelation, nor is it any longer a mystery, but rather the dissemination of the information about what was a former mystery. Therefore, if God made the mystery known to Paul by Revelation, then no other person had received the mystery prior to Paul.

  ○ "The word mystery needs a brief definition. It is not something mysterious, but it means that which was unknown, hidden from man, till it pleased God to make it known by revelation."[7]

---

7 Arno C. Gaebelein, God's Masterpiece: An Analytical Exposition of Ephesians 1–3

- The Apostles were given **the mysteries of the kingdom** (Matt. 13:11).
- Paul wanted others to know the mystery (Rom. 11:25).
- Paul states that the Gospel which we preach is **according to the revelation of the mystery** (Rom. 16:25).
- Paul declares that the mystery was **kept secret since the world began** (Rom. 16:25, Col. 1:26).
- Paul says that we are **stewards of the mysteries of God** (1 Cor. 4:1).

- When did Paul previously write about the mystery **afore in few words**? Likely this is a reference to Romans 16:25-26, where Paul did not give the means of revelation as he does here.

▸ Verse 4 - As stated in the note on v. 3, likely a reference to the mystery as mentioned in Romans 16:25. Concerning Ephesians 1:9, the mystery spoken of there is of **the dispensation of the fulness of times** (Eph. 1:10), not the mystery of the age of grace.

▸ Verse 5 –

- It seems time that the church come to realize that the mystery of Paul was **not made known** before it was revealed to Paul. The words of these verses are clear, yet the denial of them is legendary.

> "Paul says the mystery was not made known in other ages 'as it is now revealed unto his holy apostles and prophets' (Eph. 3:5). The 'as' clause may be taken either in a restrictive sense, meaning the truth was partially revealed before, or it may be taken in a descriptive sense, indicating it was totally unrevealed before. Since the

---

(New York: "Our Hope" Publication Office, 1913), 118.

same truth was declared by the same writer on another occasion (Col. 1:25-26) without the 'as' clause, it seems best to understand the phrase in Ephesians 3:5 in the descriptive sense."[8]

▶ Verse 6 –

- This is the mystery revealed! It will not only be the Jews, but also the Gentiles who are "joint-heirs," "joint-body" and "joint-partakers" of God's promise in the Messiah, through the gospel.

- The Hebrew Scriptures are filled with promises for the nations, but 100% of them are after God has glorified Israel and given her first place among the nations. There is never a hint of fellow-heirs nor that they would be of the same body. The idea of Jew and Gentile being of one Body is unheard of in the Hebrew Scriptures. That is, there is not even a hint of this dispensation prior to Paul. The prophets did not predict it, Jesus did not teach it, Peter did not proclaim it.

- Note that this does not replace the promises of God to Abraham and the nation of Israel that would come from him. This is a *new body*, not a new nation.

---

[8] Robert P. Lightner, *Christ: His Church, His Cross, His Crown* (Taos, NM: Dispensational Publishing House, 2018), 71.

EPHESIANS 3:7-12
PAUL, THE APOSTLE OF THE MYSTERY

▶ Verses 7-8 –

- Paul literally says he is a *deacon* of the Gospel. His service of the Gospel comes as a **gift of the grace of God**. While all people have the opportunity to believe, and all believers have the opportunity serve the Gospel, the wording here is unique to Paul and his calling as the apostle to the Gentiles.

- Paul declares himself to be **least of all the saints** (Jewish believers) but nonetheless the one to **preach among the Gentiles**. This is not a false humility, but a true statement due to the fact that he was a persecutor of the saints long before becoming one.

- When Paul speaks of the **unsearchable riches of Christ**, he is making reference to the mystery previously hidden (thus unsearchable).

  ○ The Greek is ἀνεξιχνίαστος [anexichniastos], the negated form of *ichnos*, which is a footprint or track. Ichnology is the study of "traces" to determine information about animals or past situations.

- If Paul says that this mystery is **unsearchable,** one wonders why so many Bible teachers find *traces* of it prior to Paul.
- Why do so many make **unsearchable** mean *beyond ability to fully comprehend?* The word has a clear meaning AND it is clear in its context:
  - Paul uses the word **mystery** (something unsearchable) in vv. 3 and 9.
  - Paul says that this mystery in other ages was not made known unto the sons of men in v. 5.
  - Paul says that the mystery **from the beginning of the world hath been hid in God** in v. 9.
  - Yet still people want to remove the clear meaning of **unsearchable**.
- Consider these translations:
  - NASB: Unfathomable
  - NLT: endless treasures
  - HCSB: incalculable riches
  - TEV: infinite riches
  - The Message: things that are way over my head, the inexhaustible riches…

▶ Verse 9 –

- Paul's first role as the last Apostle is to **preach among the Gentiles the riches of Christ** that could not previously have been preached (because they were **unsearchable**) (v. 8). His second role is to **make all…see what is the fellowship of the mystery.**
- The word **fellowship** is κοινωνία [koinonia] which is koinos (to have things in common) with the suffix -ia, which is used to

make an abstract noun out of an adjective (in English, often used with places, such as Columbia and with diseases such as malaria.)

- Paul's goal, therefore, is that we would **see** the *commonality* that is found in **the mystery**. Sadly, most Christians today are virtually ignorant of any kind of mystery having been given through Paul to our dispensation (and this ignorance filters through into their theology).
- Paul makes perfectly clear what he has previously said by saying this mystery had previously **been hid in God** and this hiding was **from the beginning of the world**, yet is now revealed in Paul.
- If there was a **mystery** that was **hid in God** but now has been revealed to Paul by revelation and Paul is preaching this mystery and wants us to have this mystery in common, then we should certainly recognize the newness of dispensation that happened with Paul and we should focus our Christian community and living around the mystery. If this is not true, then we should deny the truths of Ephesians 3 (and so many other writings of Paul).

▶ Verse 10 - Paul's work has a goal:

- The goal *concerns* the **manifold wisdom of God**.
    - Literally, *many sided*.
    - Dispensationalism is the one theology that gives attention to the *many sided* **wisdom of God**. Other forms of theology focus solely on the unity of God's wisdom. While His wisdom has unity, that unity is only understood when the various *sides* of that wisdom are known.
- The goal is *achieved* by **the church**.
    - Sadly (as noted in the previous verse), few in the church even see **the fellowship of the mystery**, let alone are they tools to make it known.

- The goal *involves* the principalities and power in heavenly *places*.
  - If the church totally understood its role in today's world and the manner of God's wisdom expressed in this dispensation, it would be of value to the *rulers* and *authorities* of this world.
  - Since the church doesn't understand it, it has been as much of the problem (or more) than it has been of the solution to the world's problems.

- Verse 11 - The church age is in the **eternal purpose** of God, but not the previous revelation of God.

- Verse 12 –

  - In Christ we have both boldness and access with confidence.
    - **Boldness** is a speech word that is literally, "every word." That is, there is no need to hold back in what is said.
    - **Access** is from a word which means "to be led in front of." This access is *proven* or *tested*, which is the root word of the Greek word translated **confidence**.
  - Notice that these two advantages come **by the faith of him**. Notice that it is not *faith in Him*, but by *His faith*. The grammar is clear that the faith *belongs to* Jesus Christ.
    - ESV - *our faith in him* - adds *our faith* when the text says *the faith* and makes it *in him* rather than *of him*. Similar in NLT, TEV, *The Message*.
    - NIV - *through faith in him*. Similar in NKJV, HCSB,
    - NET - *because of Christ's faithfulness* - correct.

EPHESIANS 3:13-21
PAUL'S DESIRE AND PRAYER

▶ Verse 13 –

- Paul's **desire** (that is, his request from them) is that they **faint not**.
  ○ The word **faint** is ἐγκακέω [enkakeo], to come into evil.
- The prayer is that the Ephesians would not become discouraged. It is the Ephesians **glory** that they remain encouraged.
- It is a praiseworthy thing to be encouraged in the face of discouragement.

▶ Verses 14-15 –

- Paul will pray **unto the Father** (always the recipient of our prayers).
- It is in the Father that **the whole family...is named**.
  ○ This likely is an understanding that all people are in ultimate submission to God, but could be more specific of the **whole** *Christian* **family,** both dead and alive.

▶ Verses 16-19 –

- Verses 16-19 are the substance of Paul's prayer request.

- He gives four requests, all based on **the riches of his glory**. The four things that Paul wants God to give to the Ephesians on this basis are:
  - Strength that comes from the **might by his Spirit** who dwells in **the inner man**. The phrase "inner man" is used in Romans 7:22 and 2 Corinthians 4:16 and is a reference to the spiritual realm of the human existence. The **might by his Spirit** is not a Samson kind of might that was in the *outer man*, but is an invisible spiritual strength.
  - Verse 17 is grammatically one request, though the KJV semicolon makes it look like two. The request is that Christ would **dwell in your hearts** both **by faith** and that your hearts would be **rooted and grounded in love**. (Note: most of the recently popular negative preaching about "asking Jesus into your hearts" is built on a Calvinism that requires works to prove salvation and is largely unrelated to this verse, though this verse is the only verse that mentions Christ in our hearts.)
  - That the Ephesians would *fully grasp* the full dimension of _____. The sentence is not completed. It could be connected with v. 19, so that the full dimension of the **love of Christ** is in view, but the grammar doesn't lend itself to this. More likely the clue is the words **with all the saints**. It was the Jewish believers who had experienced the full **breadth, and length, and depth, and height** of the work of God in the world through Jesus Christ, who walked among them. Paul's prayer is that, even though they were in a different time and place, they would have a full experience with Christ.
  - Verse 19 is one request, based on the knowing *the love of Christ, which is beyond knowledge* in order **that ye might be**

filled with all the fulness of God. Though we can never fully grasp the love of Christ, we should learn more and more to see and appreciate this love, for doing so will allow us to be *filled unto fullness* with God.

- Verses 20-21 –

  - Paul concludes his prayer with a petition of praise. It is praise because it glorifies God, it is petition because it indirectly asks for God's power in our lives.

  - Even with **the power that worketh in us,** our prayers only touch the surface of God's ability, for He can **do exceeding abundantly above all that we ask or think.**

    - Paul says *glory to Him* **in the church by Christ Jesus.**

    - The word **church** should probably be translated *assembly* since the church does not extend **throughout all ages, world without end.**

EPHESIANS 4:1-3
THE INSTRUCTIONS FOR A WORTHY WALK

- Verse 1 –
    - The word **beseech** is the familiar Greek word παρακαλέω [parakaleo], often used of the Holy Spirit. It means *to come alongside with a call*.
    - The word **worthy** is ἀξίως [axios] from which we get *axiom* and *axiomatic*. An axiom is a *self-evident truth*, and our walk is to be *axiomatic*, that is, *of the nature of self-evident truth*.
    - The word **vocation** is from the root καλεω [kaleo], thus a *calling*. Thus, this root is used three times in verse 1, in **beseech**, **vocation**, and **called**. While the modern sense of a **vocation** is a career, the fuller sense is *a calling*. Notice the *vocal* root of the word.
- Verses 2-3 –
    - The instructions of verses 2-3 are Paul's expansion of the instruction to **walk worthy**. To do so, our walk must be:

- **with all lowliness** - that is a *humble thought process*.
- **and meekness** - that is, a *gentle spirit* in all that we do.
- **with longsuffering, forbearing one another in love** - our Christian lives should lead us to have a *long fuse* before our anger bursts, and an endurance of others based on **love**.
- **endeavouring to keep the unity of the Spirit** - we should have a *diligent labor* that works toward unity. Our spirit should be, "how can I bring us together in the Spirit **in the bond of peace?**"

EPHESIANS 4:4-6
THE UNITY OF OUR BOND

The **bond of peace** (v. 3) is possible because of the *oneness* of who we are.

▶ *There is* **one body** - This **body** is *not* the church, as so many surmise. Rather, it is the *body of Christ* in heaven, into which we enter as believers. Compare Ephesians 2:16 in which **one body** is the physical body of Christ. See also Ephesians 5:30 and 1 Corinthians 12:13. (Note: If the *church* is the *body of Christ*, then either the entire church must be united together in one body or the local church is the body and there is not just one).

- There is a Biblical pattern of a *shadow* of the true thing on earth:
    - The tabernacle: Hebrews 8:5
    - The Holy Place: Hebrews 9:24
    - The Sacrifices: Hebrews 10:1
    - The elements of the Lord's Supper: Matthew 26:26-28
    - Jerusalem: Hebrews 12:22

- If there is a Biblical pattern for the *reality* in heaven and the *shadow* on earth, then why not with the body? The **one body** is in Heaven and the local church is the *shadow* of that body.

  - **one Spirit** - compare Ephesians 2:18, 22
  - **one hope of your calling** - This **hope** is the singular future to which we look forward as those who have accepted the invitation to receive salvation in Christ.
  - **one Lord** - Our head, Jesus Christ.
  - **one faith** - There is a **faith which was once delivered** (Jude 1:3) in which we have entered. The "Christian faith" is a singular faith, even when the *doctrines of the Christian church* are many and varied.
  - **one baptism** - rather than water baptism (which are many), this is the baptism into the **one body** (see 1 Cor. 12:13).
  - **one God and Father** - our **bond of peace** (v. 3) is impossible if we are not agreed on the identity and nature of God, who is
    - **above all** - literally "over" all, the One with both the perspective and the power we need.
    - **through all** - that is, He is *thoroughly everywhere.*
    - and **in you all** - God is in us and we are in Him through faith.

EPHESIANS 4:7-16
THE GRACE GIVEN FOR THE UNITY OF OUR FAITH

- Verse 7 –
  - Each one of us has the same measure of grace.
    - Grace is given according to the measure of the gift of Christ.
    - This gift of Christ is an endless fountain. Compare Romans 12:3.
  - Note that here the emphasis is on **every** while in v. 13 the emphasis is on **some**.
- Verse 8 –
  - Paul quotes from Psalm 68:18, which is a Psalm of Reign (the victory of the Messiah and His future reign).
  - The verse speaks of the then future victory over all that had been taken into **captivity**, and the day when He would take **captivity captive** (that is, gain control over it from the Satanic control it was under).
  - This victory would have taken place at the resurrection, and given in full at the Second Coming.

- Paul changes the text slightly when he says **and gave gifts unto men,** while the Hebrew says, **Thou hast received gifts for men**.
- In the Psalm, the verse goes on to speak about **the rebellious**, a reference to Israel, but Paul applies the verse to the church in the present tense.

▶ Verse 9 –

- Jesus used this same argument (to argue His divinity) in John 3:13 and 6:33. Compare also John 6:62 and 20:17.
- When Paul says that Jesus **descended first into the lower parts of the earth** he is making reference to the world of the dead (as in Ps. 63:9 and Mt. 12:40).
- While the Apostle's Creed says, "He descended into hell," hell (the lake of fire) was uninhabited at that point, and remains so today.
    - It is only populated beginning with the Second Coming.
    - Today, unbelievers go to the world of the dead and await the resurrection.
    - (Note: from this teaching some have wandered into a doctrine of "Soul Sleep," which is *non sequitur*).

▶ Verse 10 –

- The *session* of Christ is His position today, at the right hand of the Father. He has ascended **that he might fill all things**.
- The word **fill** is translated **fulfill** in 2 Thessalonians 1:11, where it is used in the exact same form. The ascension of Jesus Christ is part of fulfilling all things (Ps. 110:1).

▶ Verse 11 –

- Earlier Paul spoke of how Christ **gave gifts unto men,** but now he speaks of **some** who received *particular positions*.

- The list is not a list of *spiritual gifts*, but of *spiritual offices* that Christ has given:
  - **Apostles** - those given direct orders from Jesus Christ.
  - **Prophets** - those who received direct oracles from God.
  - **Evangelists** - those who were sent forth proclaiming the Good News.
  - **Pastors and teachers** - those assigned a role of shepherding and teaching.
- Note that this doesn't say that Christ *gives* but that **he gave**. If these positions are still given by Christ, one would have to find another passage of Scripture to prove such. Those who designate these as the "five-fold offices of the church" are doing eisegesis.

▶ Verse 12 –
- The purpose of giving these positions was for **the perfecting of the saints**.
  - Note that **perfecting** is a better translation than *equipping*.
  - The Greek καταρτισμός [katartismos] is *"the ultimate work of art."*
- The list in verse 12 is not a list of three separate things, but one building on another. It was **the saints** who did the **work of the ministry** toward the **edifying of the body of Christ**.
- In 1 Corinthians 12:27-28 Paul also speaks of the **body of Christ** in the context of gifts.
- In both 1 Corinthians 12 and in this verse, the **body** is the local church, the reflection of the physical body that is in heaven.

- Verse 13 –

  - Continuing the purpose of the giving of offices, the goal of these offices was a **unity** in both **the faith and of the knowledge** of Jesus Christ.
  - This unity will bring the local church to be **a perfect man** who displays **the measure of the stature of the fulness of Christ**.
  - That is, the local church is the perfect reflection of the body of Christ, which is in heaven.

- Verse 14 –

  - If we reach this unity and become the **perfect man** (v. 13), then we would not be **children** in faith, who display these characteristics:
    - **tossed** and carried **about with every wind of doctrine**.
    - Fooled by the **sleight of men** along with their **cunning craftiness**.
    - These two issues are among the greatest maladies in the church today.

- Verses 15-16 –

  - Rather than being tossed to and fro, and carried about (v. 14), we may grow up into him in all things when we are speaking the truth.
  - There is a good possibility that the comma should go after truth, thus "speaking the truth, in love we might grow up into him…"
  - The important matter is that we not deceive (v. 14) but speak truth.

EPHESIANS 4:17-32
PRACTICAL INSTRUCTIONS FOR OUR WALK

- Verse 17 –
  - Literally, Paul instructs the Ephesian believers not to walk as *the rest of the nations are walking*.
    - Specifically, the nations are walking **in the vanity of their mind**.
    - This is one of the reasons that the philosophy of *rationalism* must be wholly rejected in favor of a worldview that relies on *revelation*.
      - The American Heritage Dictionary defines rationalism as "the theory that the exercise of reason, rather than experience, authority, or *spiritual revelation*, provides the primary basis for knowledge" [Emphasis mine].
      - Rationalism is **vanity** because it reasons from within a closed system, without all the evidence, while assuming that it is evaluating all evidence.
  - The vanity of the mind can come from several sources in addition to the philosophy of rationalism. Several sources of this

vanity are ignorance, conceit, rigidity of thinking, rejection of evidence, etc.

- Verse 18 –

  - Those who have adopted a **vanity** of thinking have their **understanding darkened**. The word **understanding** is διάνοια [dianoia], which is literally *through thought*, and is the word from which we get *diagnosis*.

  - These people are not in fellowship with God because of their **ignorance** and they are ignorant due to the **blindness of their heart** (the word **blindness** is an interpretation, a literal translation would be *hardness*).

  - Note that they are not **alienated from the life of God** by election, but by blindness and ignorance. Our job as evangelists is to help them to see the **vanity of their mind** (v. 17).

- Verse 19 –

  - The verb **being past feeling** is in the active tense, meaning that they have "*cast off all feeling*" (Darby Translation). Having done this, they then give themselves to **all uncleanness with greediness**.

  - It is a dangerous thing to become morally callous.

- Verses 20-21 –

  - Those who believe have **learned Christ** in a different manner than those of vain thinking (who have also learned of Christ, whose fame is beyond the ability to claim ignorance in every part of the world that has any contact with other parts of the world).

  - If you have **heard him, and have been taught by him** (through the Scriptures), then you have the **truth** about Him.

- Verse 22 –

  - These are simple instructions. Because a believer has **learned Christ** (v. 20) and **heard him** and **been taught by him** (v. 21) the believer is to live differently than before.

  - The believer is to **put off** (v. 22), **be renewed** (v. 23), and **put on** (v. 24).

  - Note the following concerning v. 22:

    - This is a *repentance* of behavior, and is a *result of* not a *path to* belief in Christ.

    - The word **conversation** has changed in the English language, losing its connection to its Latin root: *con vertere* (with a turn). The Latin closely matches the Greek ἀναστροφή [anastrophe] (*turning again*). The modern sense of the word did not come about until almost 1800. Thus, the instruction is to rid yourself of the *turning round and round* that the **old man** did.

    - The **old man** (before learning of Christ and being taught by Him) was **corrupt** with a corruption that came from **deceitful lusts**. The Greek is literally *the lusts that belong to deceit*. The lusts are real, but they were created by the deceit of the deceiver, Satan himself.

- Verse 23 –

  - Since there is an **old man** (v. 22) that has now come to faith, he is to **be renewed in the spirit of your mind**.

    - Paul doesn't give a step-by-step outline of how to achieve this renewal, possibly because it would be different for each person (or because we should learn to figure out some things for ourselves).

- However, grammatically, Paul is not commanding the believer to **be renewed**, but showing this as a result of the verbs of vv. 20-21.
  - The verses can be displayed as follows:
    - You **learned**, you **heard**, and you were **taught** (vv. 20-21) *for the purpose of* putting off, being renewed, and putting on (vv. 22-24).
    - Each of the verbs in vv. 20-21 are in the indicative (a statement of fact) and each of the verbs in vv. 22-24 are in the infinitive (which requires a preceding verb).

▶ Verse 24 –

- As with the preceding "instructions," this is a *result*.
  - However, one should not assume that because these are results that they do not require personal action.
  - One must participate in and cooperate with the verbs of vv. 20-21 in order to achieve the results of vv. 22-24.
- The **new man** for which we have **learned Christ** (etc.), is a man that has **God** as its pattern. Therefore, when we ask, "what manner of man shall I be?" we should look to God (whom we see through Jesus) for the answer.

▶ Verse 25 –

- In vv. 25-32 we find direct commands to the one who is now a **new man.**
- The commands begin with **wherefore**, which is a translation of *dia*, thus could be translated, *through this* (the instructions above) now **put away lying**, etc.

- Literally, the Greek says, *having put away lying, speak truth....* It is assumed by Paul that the **new man** would have put away lying as a part of his old **conversation**.
- Paul instructs that we should **speak...truth** because of our interconnectedness. None of us is an island unto himself.

▶ Verse 26 –

- This verse is most often misinterpreted (and very often mistranslated) to teach that anger is a sin. In reality, the *instruction* is to **be ye angry,** and to do so before sundown.
- This is part of speaking truth, as instructed in v. 25.

▶ Verse 27 –

- Because the word **neither** is a negative conjunction, it must be connected with the previous phrase concerning sundown.
- Invariably, if one harbors anger rather than expressing it, it will **give place to the devil** either by allowing the sin to continue or allowing the anger to build up to dangerous levels.

▶ Verse 28 –

- Paul uses the illustration of thievery to display the change of behavior that should take place in a believer.
- Those who **stole** should **steal no more** rather *labor productively with hands* in order that **he may have to give to him that needeth**.

▶ Verse 29 –

- The word **corrupt** is σαπρός [sapros].
  - In English, a *saprophyte* is a "bacteria or fungus that grows on decaying organic matter." The words that would grow off decay rather than **to the use of edifying** are to be avoided by believers.

- Notice that the KJV uses **communication** rather than **conversation**, as in v. 22, showing the precision of the KJV English.
- Do the words you speak *build up* and **minister grace unto the hearers**? This can be done even when the words are words of anger (v. 26).

▶ Verse 30 –

- Rather than deep speculation about what grieves the **holy Spirit of God,** we can take our first instincts if we have any Biblical concept of God at all. If it grieves God the Father or God the Son, it grieves God the Spirit.
- In Ephesians 1:13 the sealing of the Holy Spirit was the first mention Paul gave concerning gentile believer's benefits.
  - While the Jewish nation was given the **earnest of our inheritance until the redemption of the purchased possession** (Eph. 1:14), the believer is given the *seal* of the Spirit.
  - In Revelation 7 we have the advance-record of the physical sealing of 144,000, to the extent that nothing could harm them.
  - The spiritual sealing of the believer must certainly be of the same nature, so that nothing can *spiritually* harm the believer (who is complete in Christ).
  - The hymn, *A Mighty Fortress Is Our God* displays this truth in poetic form.
- The Spirit was given in *earnest* on the day of Pentecost, and in *sealing* at the time of an individual's belief.

▶ Verse 31 –

- While there is a *general* truth to this statement, if it is not read *specifically* a contradiction is created with verse 26.

- How can the Apostle instruct his audience to **be ye angry** (v. 26) and to **put away** their **anger** in this verse?
- When read carefully, the verse does *not* ask *all people* to **put away** the **bitterness, and wrath, and anger, and clamour, and evil speaking**.
  - Rather, he is addressing **you, with all malice**.
  - One must recognize that **malice** is not an additional vice to put away, but rather a *description of those to whom the command is addressed.* The word **malice** is in the dative case.
  - One Greek scholar says, "The true dative is used to designate the person more remotely concerned"[9]
  - Note that 2 Corinthians 2:4 uses the same English form, saying **you with many tears**. However, in this passage the word **tears** substitutes **wrath** and is in the *genitive*, an adjective describing Paul. Had the words been in the *dative*, they would have described the recipients.
  - In 2 Corinthians 12:16 Paul says **I caught you with guile**. Here the word **guile** is in the dative, and describes **you**.
- Sadly, most modern translations confuse the grammar and add words such as "along with," making **malice** an additional item on the list.

▸ Verse 32 - There is always room for kindness, tenderheartedness, and forgiveness. If our lives are simply anger, doctrinal purity, and moral righteousness, we forget the tremendous grace that God has given us in Christ.

---

9 The Berean Christian Bible Study Resources, (2009, Feb. 10). Retrieved from http://www.bcbsr.com/greek/gcase.html

EPHESIANS 5:1-14
MORAL CHRISTIAN BEHAVIOR

▶ Verse 1 –

- Paul asks the congregation to be **followers of God**. The word **followers** is μιμητής [mimates], an *imitator*. Believers should *imitate* God in behavior as God's **dear children**

- Note that since each of the commands in chapter 5 is in the plural, there is a sense in which the *church* must consider how to do this collectively (which requires individual involvement). See v. 24 which says, **as the church is**…

▶ Verse 2 –

- This is one of three "as Christ also" statements in the Bible.

    ○ Romans 5:17 - **receive one another, as Christ also**…

    ○ Ephesians 5:2 - **walk in love, as Christ also**…

    ○ Ephesians 5:25 - **love your wives, as Christ also**…

- Note that all three of them use Christ as the *standard* for interpersonal relations.

- Jesus became **an offering** (that which did not involve blood) and **a sacrifice** (that which required blood) **to God**.

- It is important to recognize that any theology of the ministry of Jesus that only sees Him as an example is insufficient, and any Christology that only sees Him as a **sacrifice** is equally insufficient. Christ is our example, both an **offering** to us in His life, ministry, and example, and a **sacrifice** for us in His death.
- Now, in resurrected life, His **sacrifice** is an **offering** to us. Having accepted this as the basis for our salvation, our lives should be a **sweetsmelling savour**.

▶ Verse 3 –

- In verses 3-5, Paul gives sinful activity that should **not be once named among you.**
  - **Fornication** is an inclusive word for sexual sins. **Uncleanness** is *that which is not kathartic* (purifying or cleansing), using the word ἀκαθαρσία [akatharsia]. Thus, if an activity *fuels the fires of sin* then it should not be part of our activity. The word **covetousness** is based on two Greek roots which mean "to have more."
  - While these three may be taken individually, it looks like Paul intends to include **uncleanness or covetousness** with **fornication** because he uses the **let it not once be named** rather than *let THEM not once be named*. Thus Darby translates all three as related, "But fornication and all uncleanness or unbridled lust, let it not be even named…"
- When Paul says, **as becometh saints** he uses the Jews under the Law, which has clear and strong instruction to moral behavior, as the standard. He is *not* claiming that the Ephesians are **saints**. The word **becometh** means, *is fitting*.

- ▶ Verse 4 –
  - Adding to the previous list, Paul adds three things which (with the possible exception of the first) are related to our speech.
    - **Filthiness** is only used here in the New Testament, and likely refers to *obscenity*.
    - **Foolish talking** is μωρολογία [morologia], built on the root *moros*, which is *foolish* (and from which we get words like *moronic*).
    - Added to this is **jesting** (also used only here in the New Testament) which is literally a "good turn" of a phrase, but is used in a negative light, meaning to "twist words" so that they lose objective meaning.
  - These three (plural) are said to be **not convenient**. The Greek means "not appropriate." The English sense of "avoiding difficulty" did not enter the English language until the 1600s, thus later translations use words like "not fitting."
  - Rather than obscenity, moronic speech, twisting and turning words, our speech should be characterized by **giving of thanks**.
- ▶ Verse 5 –
  - In verse 5, Paul momentarily goes from speaking to the church to speaking of the individual.
  - When Paul speaks of **whoremonger** or **unclean person** or **covetous man**, he uses root words that he has previously used in v. 3.
    - Paul adds the words, **who is an idolater** to the list, and the grammar allows this to be a qualifier for the entire list (as in KJV) or the last item on the list (as in ESV).

- It is important to recognize that Paul is *not* speaking to a believer's salvation, but rather using the Jewish people under the law (as in v. 3) as a comparison.
  - The believer has no **inheritance** in the Kingdom or otherwise, but is given a *free gift* that is not based on any legal standing (the word **inheritance** is inextricably intertwined with legality).
  - Those who take this verse to mean that none of the above list can go to heaven necessarily have to build a "Lordship" salvation theology that says that a professing believer is not a true believer if they have any form of these sins in their lives.

▶ Verse 6 –

- The church must be on guard for **vain words** (literally, words that have been drained of meaning, they are *empty words*).
- Likely, Paul had someone in mind who was teaching a *libertine* theology that said that **these things** spoken in previous verses were acceptable in the church.
- Paul wanted to remind them that *through* (dia) **these things cometh the wrath of God**.
- While the word *dia* could be **because of**, it can more forcefully be said that God's wrath comes *through* these things.

▶ Verse 7 - The church should not partner **with them**, both a reference to the **children of disobedience** (v. 6) and the activities mentioned in vv. 1-6.

▶ Verse 8 –

- Paul continues to speak to the congregation, giving testimony which is true of the whole because it is the experience of the individual.

- Thus, those of the congregation who are now **light in the Lord** should not take pride over those who are just coming out of their **darkness**.
- Each of us should provide encouragement to **walk as children of light**, for it is easy to slip back into darkness.
- Note that the Greek word translated **sometimes** is an *indefinite particle*, so that it could mean "at one time in the past" but could just as easily mean "sometimes now and sometimes even into the future."
- If the word doesn't continue to mean **sometimes** then the encouragement is moot, for our walking in darkness would be wholly past.
- Since we are still **sometimes darkness** we need to hear and heed this instruction (which concludes in v. 10, with a parenthetical in v. 9).

▶ Verse 9 - Paul will not elaborate on the **fruit of the Spirit** until the next chapter. However, here he says that this fruit is found in **all goodness and righteousness and truth**. Therefore, when we are involved in any of these, we are in the in the "fruit orchard."

▶ Verse 10 –
- Our walking **as children of light** is **proving** (showing to be genuine) the things which are **acceptable unto the Lord**.
- Note that our righteous walk doesn't prove that something is **acceptable unto the Lord**, but rather takes what is **acceptable unto the Lord** and proves it to be the righteous and honorable way to live.
    - The NASB and ESV translations, "trying to learn" and "try to discern," respectively, give a "trial and error" approach to discovering that which is acceptable unto the Lord.

- The concept of the language, it appears to me, is that **proving what is acceptable** (v. 10) is the result of walking **as children of light** (v. 8).

▶ Verse 11 –

- While perhaps a minor point, the instruction is to avoid **the unfruitful works** and not *the workers* of darkness.
- It would be difficult to avoid fellowship with these works while fellowshipping with the workers, but the instruction (at least in this verse) is for **unfruitful works**.
- Paul gives no list to tell us exactly what these works are, so discernment is clearly necessary.
  - John 3:19-21 connects the one who **hateth the light** with the one who **doeth evil**, saying that the one with the evil actions hates light because the light will cause his **deeds** to be **reproved**.
  - In the end, the Bible is concerned with *actions*, and it is the act that is reproved, not the actor (who always has room to repent), as Paul encouraged in Romans 13:12.
- To **reprove** is to *expose*.
  - The believer does not fellowship with **works of darkness** but exposes them.
  - He/she can expose these works in such a way that it allows the one doing the work to repent, preferably privately.
  - There is no need to expose the *worker* if he/she repents of the *work*.
  - Therefore, we should seek to expose:
    - Alcoholism, but not the alcoholic.
    - Adultery, but not the adulterer.
    - Greed, but not the greedy, etc.

- To do this is to allow room for restoration (which should be our motive, otherwise we are fellowshipping with **unfruitful works of darkness**).

▶ Verse 12 - The heart of this sentence (in support of the previous claim that we avoid *works* not *workers*) is "the things (being done by them in secret) it is shameful to say."

▶ Verse 13 –

- Once again, it is the **things that are reproved** and not *the people that are reproved*. If there is a way to expose *works* and protect *workers of darkness*, we must first attempt to do so.

- These **things...are made manifest by the light**. This is why we are to **walk as children of light** (v. 8).

- This passage defines **light** as **whatsoever doth make manifest**.

- Note that modern translations based on the Critical Text (put together by German rationalists) divide verses 13-14 differently, and change the fundamental meaning. Thus ESV reads, "But when anything is exposed by the light, it becomes visible, 14 for anything that becomes visible is light..."

▶ Verse 14 –

- The quote appears to begin with the word **awake** and end with **light**. However, there is no known direct quote, so it could be more, or less.

- This could be a well-known saying, a saying by someone in the congregation, something written in a book, or a quote from God given directly to Paul as he wrote.

EPHESIANS 5:15-21
THE BELIEVER'S SPIRITUAL WALK

▶ Verse 15 - The congregation is implored to **walk circumspectly** (i.e. carefully, accurately). The walk is to be with wisdom, not foolishness (The Greek is not *a-sophia* but with *sophia*).

▶ Verse 16 –

- The word **redeeming** is ἐξαγοράζω [exagorazo], from *ex* (out of) and *agora* (the central marketplace).
  - *Agoraphobia* is a "fear of open places,"
  - *Allegory* is *another* (allos) *agora*
  - *Category* is "the whole marketplace.").
- The instruction is to *take your time out of the marketplace* with the implication of using it elsewhere because **the days are evil**.
- Each of us should analyze our time and ask if our time is used in a *wise* manner. A love of wisdom in the use of our time does not mean we should "burn the candle at both ends," but should remind us that in these evil days that some use of time is "aiding and abetting the enemy" or is simply time that will not have any positive accomplishment.

- Verse 17 –

  - The word **wherefore** is connected with **redeeming the time** (v. 16) and is literally *through this* **be ye not unwise**. That is, in the redemption of time, believers should, with wisdom, **understand what the will of the Lord is**.

  - Another possibility is that the verse says that *when we redeem the time we will not be unwise but we will understand what the will of the Lord is.*

- Verse 18 –

  - Anywhere that alcoholic beverage is served, drunkenness can be a problem. Drunkenness goes against the wise redemption of time, and thus is prohibited for believers.

  - To be **drunk with wine** is **excess**. One should rather be **filled with the Spirit**.

  - While Paul never gives a step-by-step approach, he does give some insight in vv. 19-21.

- Verses 19-21 –

  - The command is to **be filled with the Spirit** (v. 18), and Paul gives five activities that should be done by those who are filled:

    - **Speaking to yourselves in psalms and hymns and spiritual songs**. It would be going beyond the meaning of language to divide these rigidly into different types of music. The point should be that our communication to one another should have a musical element.

    - **Singing and making melody** could be taken as aspects of **speaking**, or as two separate activities.

    - **Giving thanks always**. A life of thanksgiving should characterize the one who is filled with the Spirit.

- Incidentally, in KJV English *alway* is different from **always**.
- The word *always* is "on every occasion" whereas *alway* is "perpetually."
- Alway is used 23 times in the KJV, and always is used 62 times.
- Philippians 4:4 says **rejoice in the Lord alway**.
  ○ **Submitting yourselves one to another** is the final activity, and this submission is done **in the fear of God**, thus is never done in a manner which would offend God.
- A group of believers who does these five activities as their spiritual DNA would be easily set apart from other groups of the world.

▶ Summary of vv. 15-21: The section began with a command to walk **circumspectly** (that is, with accuracy, carefully, precisely). It then gave insight into a circumspect walk:

- Each step is taken with wisdom (v. 15).
- Wisdom helps us pull our time away from the evils of the "marketplace" and use it for God's glory and our own wellbeing (v. 16).
- As we redeem our time, we discover the will of God for our lives (v. 17).
- Our *spirit* is to be the Holy Spirit, who fills us, meeting the need that some, having lack, use alcoholic *spirits* to fill (v. 18).
- Being filled with the Spirit, our lives are characterized by music, thanksgiving, and mutual submission.

EPHESIANS 5:22-33
THE BELIEVER'S MARRIAGE RELATIONSHIP

Note: while some prefer to connect v. 21 with vv. 22 and following due to the submission of v. 21, the grammar puts the four participles of vv. 19-21 together with the instruction to **be filled** in v. 18.

▶ Verse 22 –

- Wives now become the subject of the new sentence, and they are to **submit** themselves to their **husbands** (or *men*, in the case of an unmarried woman to her father, as the Greek word is *women* or *wives* and *husbands* or *men* only by context).

- The Greek word translated **submit yourselves** is ὑποτάσσω [hupotasso], which means "to come under the order of." Order, as in *orderly*.

- This is to be done **as unto the Lord**.

  ○ It is significant to remember that neither a woman nor a man would submit to the Lord in a self-destructive nor sinful manner, nor is a woman instructed to do so here to her husband.

- It is also significant that parts of the world that have been influenced by Judeo-Christian thinking are the same areas that treat women with dignity and respect.
- Far from being a "Neanderthal" instruction that is demeaning to women, this instruction provides a place of dignity and freedom for women.

- How does a woman submit **unto the Lord**?
  - Voluntarily, as a response to His love and grace.
  - Totally, as an expression of her faith.
  - As a Berean, searching for the truth.

▶ Verse 23 -

- There has, from the beginning, been a God-given authoritative role for the man, and his role is one of dominion over the created order.
  - God's authoritative structure was always:

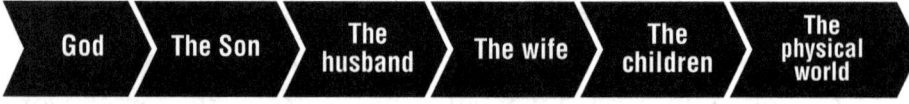

God › The Son › The husband › The wife › The children › The physical world

- From the beginning, man has flipped this order. The temptation and fall in the Garden was the total opposite of God's plan. Since this time, man has continually come under the dominion of the physical creation (both by his own choices and by the forces of nature, which are a result of the curse), and male/female relationships have suffered from brutality (especially in non-Judeo-Christian societies) or feminism.
- Paul also speaks of the order of men and women in 1 Corinthians 11:1-14.

- ▶ Verse 24 –
  - In similar fashion to v. 22, Paul now uses **the church** as the example of being **subject**, showing that subjection is not *Neanderthal* nor *humiliating.*
  - Once again, one must ask, "in what manner is the church subject to Christ?" And, once again, one finds that the church is subject to Christ in a voluntary submission that grows out of her love and respect and gratitude for the grace shown through Christ.
- ▶ Verse 25 –
  - Naturally, the love of the husband comes out of the conversation, since the relationship of Christ and His church entered into the conversation.
  - True love is always a giving love. Christ's love for **the church** motivated Him to give **himself,** and this giving kind of love is what a husband is called to give to his wife.
- ▶ Verse 26 –
  - Literally, "he gave Himself, in order that, having cleansed it, He might sanctify it…"
  - The cleansing came from the sacrifice Christ made, the sanctification comes from the **washing of water by the word.**
  - This phrase is somewhat mysterious.
    - The Greek for **word** is ῥῆμα [rhema], which is the *spoken* word.
    - In John's Gospel, after the washing of the feet, Jesus said, **ye are clean** (Jn. 13:10), and on the same occasion said **ye are clean through the word which I have spoken unto you** (Jn. 15:3).

- The reference to the upper room makes it plausible that the *ecclesia* spoken of is the *Jewish assembly*, but making that application would not materially change the point being made (though it might spare us from making the false conclusion that the church is the Bride of Christ).
- This verse does not speak of water baptism.

▶ Verse 27 –

- This verse gives a second **that he might** statement, both being built upon the fact that Christ cleansed the *ecclesia*.
- The second statement is **that he might present it to himself**.
    - Paul wants to present the church to Christ (2 Cor. 11:2), but this is different than Christ presenting an assembly *to Himself*.
    - This gives added credence to the position that the *ecclesia* is the Jewish nation.
    - Furthermore, the words **holy and without blemish** are words rich with meaning in the old Covenant, and thus very appropriate if redeemed Israel is in mind.

▶ Verse 28 –

- As previously noted, whether Paul had the Jewish *assembly* in mind or the *church*, the application remains the same, and is restated here using the illustration of a man's love for his own body.
- Paul then makes a reverse application, saying, **He that loveth his wife loveth himself**. A man's self-esteem (or lack thereof) can be seen in his love for his wife.

▶ Verse 29 - Even a man who is not satisfied with his body still **nourisheth and cherisheth it** (for it is the only one he has). The example of Christ's care for **the church** is given once again, this time as a supporting example.

- Verse 30 - This verse is the best evidence that **the church** (vv. 25, 27, 29) is *not* a reference to the Jewish assembly, for Paul uses the pronoun **we** to speak of the **members of his body**. However, one could argue that Paul is using the first person plural in the same manner as chapters 1-2, which would then revert the argument to the Jewish assembly. Note that **we are members** of Christ's *physical* body (**of his flesh, and of his bones**) because we are "in Christ."

- Verse 31 - The verse begins with the Greek word Ἀντὶ [anti], a pronoun that literally means "in the place of" (as the *antithesis* is something that is trying to *take the place of* the thesis). Thus, "in the place of" being **members of his body** (v. 30) the husband and wife marriage relationship is to serve as a living example of this "oneness" to the world.

- Verse 32 - From this verse some make the false conclusion that the church is the bride of Christ. Rather, the **great mystery** is how **two shall be one flesh** (v. 31). Paul here emphasizes that in vv. 29-32 the unity of the church has been the topic, with the marriage as an example.

- Verse 33 - This verse is perhaps the greatest summary for a good marriage that can be found in the Bible. Wives need the **love** of their husbands and husbands need the **reverence** of their wives.

EPHESIANS 6:1-4
THE RESPONSIBILITY OF BELIEVING CHILDREN AND PARENTS

▶ Verse 1 –

- While wives were to **submit** (5:23), children are to **obey**.
- The fact that the Scripture uses a different word sheds insight on the role of the wife.
    - Note: the command to promise to "obey" came into the English weddings in the first book of Common Prayer in 1549 (the same year as the "Act of Uniformity" that changed church services from Latin to English in the Anglican Church).
        - The Scripture does not require wives to obey, but to submit.
        - The Greek word **submit** has the idea of "rank" or "order" (see note on v. 23) while the word **obey** is ὑπακούω [hupoakuo], "to come under the hearing" (and thus heed what your hear).
- The phrase **in the Lord** and **for this is right** could be put together to say, "this is right in the Lord." That is, for children who are **in the Lord** the **right** thing to do is **obey your parents**.

- Verses 2-3 –
  - Paul quotes Exodus 20:12, with a parenthetical note concerning **the first commandment with promise**.
  - However, Paul removed the last words of the commandment, **which the Lord thy God giveth thee**, to make this applicable to all believers.
    - Note that both in Hebrew and Greek the word for *land* and *earth* is the same word.
  - This is an example of one of the times in which Paul takes something from the Old Testament law and makes it applicable for today.
- Verse 4 –
  - Because there is an *order* in the home, with the **fathers** as the leaders of the home, the father has a great responsibility to lead wisely.
  - Harsh leadership is regularly condemned in Scripture, both by explicit teaching and by narrative.
  - The word παροργίζω [parorgizo] is literally *to come alongside wrath* and has no English equivalent.
    - In effect, it tells the father to *use a different tool* than the tool of anger/wrath. The tool to use is **the nurture and admonition of the Lord.**
      - The Greek word for **nurture** παιδεία [paideia] is an all-encompassing word for the training of a child, mentally, physically, and spiritually.
      - The Greek word for **admonition** νουθεσία [nouthesia] is "to put their thinking in order."

EPHESIANS 6:5-9
THE RESPONSIBILITY OF BELIEVING SERVANTS AND MASTERS

▶ Verse 5 –

- The word translated **servants** is δοῦλος [doulos].
  - The KJV *interpreted* the word for life in England at the time, where slavery proper had largely (not wholly) ceased to exist, and *serfdom* was the common form of servitude.
  - According to English laws at the time, a person was not considered *property* and thus "slave" was not a relevant term.
  - The word itself, however, is a slave in its more traditional understanding, as slavery did exist in 1st Century Ephesus (and throughout the Roman Empire), though not in a manner totally equivalent to slavery in Colonial America or modern Islamic slave markets.
- The word **masters** κύριος [kurios] is the same word translated **Lord**, often used in reference to Jesus Christ, but here clearly a reference to earthly **masters according to the flesh**.
  - Rather than condemn slavery Paul instructed the slaves how to relate to their masters (and vice-versa).

- This should not be taken to mean that Paul condoned slavery. Rather, he was speaking pragmatically about the fact of life in the Roman empire.
  - The slave is to **be obedient** (the same word as used for children). This obedience was to be **with fear and trembling, in singleness of your heart** and done **as unto Christ**.
  - In cases like this, the application can only come indirectly, and could be applied (though not dogmatically) to the employee/employer relationship.

▸ Verses 6-7 –

  - These verses continue with the manner in which slaves were to **be obedient**. Their obedience was **not with eyeservice** ὀφθαλμοδουλία [ophlamodoulia], literally, "slavery only when one was watching," nor as **menpleasers** but as slaves **of Christ**, and doing the **service** with **good will**.

▸ Verse 8 –

  - This verse contains an amazing promise, that all good work will be rewarded **of the Lord** both for **bond or free** (the word **bond** is also *doulos*, slave).
  - No further teaching is given as to how the Lord will repay **whatsoever good thing any man doeth**, but the promise remains nonetheless.

▸ Verse 9 –

  - As with wives and husbands (5:22-33), children and fathers (6:1-4), now Paul moves from servant to master, requiring of them laudable leadership, namely the releasing (literal translation) of **threatening**.

- The **masters** were to know that they have a **Master** who is **in heaven** and that this Master has no **respect of persons with him** (i.e.: He is not impressed by rank).

EPHESIANS 6:10-18:
THE ARMOR OF GOD

- Verse 10 –
  - Paul comes to his closing thoughts with the imperative to **be strong** with a strength that comes from being **in the Lord** as well as **the power of his might**.
  - The word **strong** is from δυναμαι [dynamai] and a reference to strength of all kinds.
  - The word **power** is κρατος [kratos], the source of many "power" words in the English language -*cracy* and -*crat* words come from *kratos* (such as democracy, Theocracy, autocrat, etc.).
- Verse 11 –
  - In order to **be strong in the Lord** (v. 10) we must put on God's armor.
    - Jesus warned the Jewish nation that **a strong man armed keepeth his palace** (Lk. 11:21) but there was the danger of **a stronger than he** that would come and **taketh from him all his armour** (Lk, 11:22). This illustrates the reason

we need **the whole armor of God** rather than some other form of protection.

- The purpose of the armor of God is to **stand against the wiles of the devil**.
    - The Greek word for **wiles** is μεθοδεία [methodeia] from *meta* (to change) and *hodos* (the *way* or *path*). The devil has *changing paths*, but by the **whole armour of God** we are able to **stand against** his *methods*.

▶ Verse 12 –

- Our struggle is **not against flesh and blood**. This theme is given several times in the New Testament.
    - Flesh and blood is not the source of revelation of Jesus as the Messiah (Mt. 16:17).
    - Flesh and blood cannot inherit the Kingdom (1 Cor. 15:50).
    - Paul did not consult with flesh and blood (Gal. 1:16).
    - Christ took the form of flesh and blood so that **he might destroy him that had the power of death** (which is the consummate "flesh and blood" problem) (Heb. 2:14).
- Our struggle is against:
    - **Principalities** - from ἀρχή [arche], the "things at the beginning." That is, against things which pre-date **flesh and blood**.
    - **Rulers of the darkness** - from κοσμοκράτωρ [kosmokrator], including *cosmos* and *krator* (see note on v. 10). Since this is plural, it is likely a reference to those whom the Devil uses in his work in this world.

- ○ **Spiritual wickedness in high** *places* - There is a wickedness that goes beyond **flesh and blood**, and goes beyond **this world**. The **spiritual wickedness** from *the heavenlies* is of greater concern.
- Note: some use this passage to claim that "our enemy is not really our enemy." This deflects arguments for "go along and get along" kind of people, but is unrelated to this verse. There are *flesh and blood* enemies. For those enemies, other passages of Scripture would be needed as the insight.

▶ Verse 13 –

- The English word **armor** implies defense. However, the Greek word implies any kind of weapon, defense or offense.
- The goal is to be able to **withstand** (literally, *stand against*, an offensive term) **in the evil day**. What day is this?
  - ○ The "day of the Lord" is "great and terrible" but not **evil**. Furthermore, the believer does not **withstand** that day because of his efforts.
  - ○ Rather, this must be a reference to "the day" in which we live, one which is characterized by **evil**. We must "do all" in order **to stand**.

▶ Verses 14-17 –

- It is possible that more has been made of these words than the words actually say.
- Rather than myopic focus on the details of armory, it would be better to see this as an illustration that focuses the reader's attention on **truth, righteousness**, the **gospel, faith, salvation**, and **the word of God**.

- Verse 18 –
  - **Praying** is as much a part of taking God's armor as girting loins, shodding feet, and the taking of shields and helmets and swords.
  - The prayer here is focused on **watching…the saints**, and doing so **with all perseverance** as well as **supplication.**
  - (If, as I have proposed, the **saints** are the Jewish believers, then we are given encouragement to *watch and pray* for them because in this **evil day** the devil's *method* has always concerned removing the Jew and the Jewish nation from this earth. To do so is the only real evil that would thwart the coming plan of God.)

EPHESIANS 6:19-20:
PRAYER FOR PAUL

- Verse 19 –
  - Of all the things Paul could pray for, he asks that "a word" **may be given unto me** in order to **make known the mystery of the gospel** with boldness.
  - There is no place in Scripture where a **mystery** is something *hard to understand* or something for which understanding comes *with investigation*. The word always means *something which was previously unknown but now made known by revelation*.
  - Since the saving Gospel is made known in the prophets and is *never* considered a mystery (1 Cor. 15:1-4), it cannot be said that Paul is praying for the word with which to share **the gospel**, but rather it is **the mystery of the gospel** which he wants to share boldly.
  - What is **the mystery of the gospel**? It is that God is offering individual immediate salvation as a grace-gift to anyone, anywhere, anytime. This is a *mystery* that cannot be found prior to God's revelation to Paul, nor will it be found after the

rapture of the church and the end of this *mystery age*, until it is restored again in the prophetic program.

▶ Verse 20 –

- Paul is **an ambassador** "in a chain" (literal translation). This could refer to literal imprisonment or the fact that Paul considers himself a **prisoner of Jesus Christ** (not *for* Jesus Christ) (Eph. 3:1).

- If the latter is the intended meaning, then **therein** refers to his bondage to Christ (thus, **woe to me if I preach not the Gospel**, 1 Cor. 9:16). In this bondage he speaks **boldly** and carries out his ambassadorship well.

EPHESIANS 6:21-24
CLOSING WORDS

▶ Verses 21-22 –

- Paul would send **Tychicus** to the Ephesians to report on the conditions and activity of Paul, and to encourage the Ephesians. Likely Tychicus would be the one to give the letter to the Ephesians.

- This **beloved brother and faithful minister** is mentioned five times in Scripture, most often as Paul's emissary (see Col. 4:7, 2 Tim. 4:12, and Titus 3:12. Also mentioned in Acts 20:4).

- Many believe that Tychicus was a native of Ephesus due to his association with Trophimus, who is known to be of Ephesus. He was the courier of at least three of Paul's letters (Ephesians, Philemon, and Colossians) and perhaps four (2 Corinthians).

▶ Verses 23-24 - Paul's closing comments are for **peace, love, faith**, and **grace** to the Ephesians, with special emphasis on **them that love our Lord Jesus Christ in sincerity**.

Dispensational Publishing House is striving to become the go-to source for Bible-based materials from the dispensational perspective.

Our goal is to provide high-quality doctrinal and worldview resources that make dispensational theology accessible to people at all levels of understanding.

Visit our blog regularly to read informative articles from both known and new writers.

And please let us know how we can better serve you.

Dispensational Publishing House, Inc.
PO Box 3181
Taos, NM 87571

Call us toll free 844-321-4202

www.DispensationalPublishing.com

www.ingramcontent.com/pod-product-compliance
Lightning Source LLC
Chambersburg PA
CBHW052159110526
44591CB00012B/2004